# "CHALK OUTLINE THESE THOUGHTS"

Robert Standish

*edytha*

ISBN 978-0-9881440-4-0



Published by *edytha*
edytha.com
Toronto, Ontario, Canada


Cover by Robert Standish

This collection is dedicated to everyone that has never taken the time to write down the brief moments of clarity.

# "CHALK OUTLINE THESE THOUGHTS"

How To Cope With A Planet That's Trying To Kill You

*Patience is the hardest lesson for most to learn, but if done right, it offers the greatest rewards.*

*Failure is everyone's right.*

*Failure is the easiest thing anyone can do; the guaranteed way is to quit.*

# "CHALK OUTLINE THESE THOUGHTS"

How To Cope With A Planet That's Trying To Kill You

*True signs of getting older – seeing, hearing and smelling things that are not there.*

*Aging is nature's way of streamlining your usefulness.*

*The only way hell works is if you are aware of your reality.*

*Heaven and Hell are interpretations of a concept that is described for us to better perceive in our own way, based on nothing tangible. The interesting part is that the reward and punishment is based on our mortal understanding of an immortal concept which we don't even understand or can prove.*

*The ultimate truth only exists where the sun shines the brightest.*

*If you don't stand for anything you will fall for nothing.*

*Justice is never served by a life sentence; when there is no way to measure the potential of the life lost by the one that replaces it.*

*Love is blind, but it does not look away. Without a glance it can stare you right in the face.*

*Just because you are holding hands doesn't mean you are both walking in the same direction.*

*Your imagination is the limit to your own immortality.*

*We have been playing God for so long that we don't even see the tragedy we create.*

*Progress happens when a question answered only brings on more questions.*

*We only offer limited help to someone else's cause.*

*Life is only good depending on your perspective.*

---

*The shortest distance between two points is a straight line but success is often never recognized the same way (simple and straight).*

*The only thing that makes torture effective is the strength of the victim's instinct and desire to survive.*

*Life is not one long breath to be taken at one time; but a series of small ones to be enjoyed more than the one before, and taken slowly and methodically. Embrace them all.*

*The religions we create cause us to separate.*

*All forms of life on earth wage War, but we are the only ones that invent the reasons.*

*We create God in our image.*

*Horses are only knobble because they can run faster than cows. How fast would a horse run if he knew the risk of a broken leg?*

*No matter how big the picture is we all see it differently.*

*The knowledge of the old should be the wisdom of the young. Allow the experience of the righteous be your guide.*

*The evolution of mankind advances the ability to destroy the planet and conserve the things that should be extinct.*

*We play God every day.*

*Mortality is the human struggle to hold onto the familiar while our survival instinct makes us fight to be immortal.*

*Science confirms what Religion can't prove. Science is the force that advances society and Religion offers the promise of comfort for the soul.*

*Therefore, science will move us forward to a time when it will test our faith. Science will prove that faith in Religion is not misguided. As energy cannot be destroyed but converted, the energy of life changes when the body expires. Hand in hand science will prove the faith of religion as soon as we figure out where to look for the next step in the cycle beyond life.*

*Death has a colour. It can best be described as pure white. Just like pure light it has equal parts of every conceivable colour equally mixed together. It begins to change once our eyes adjust to it and we can begin to see each colour for what it is. This is just like the emotional rollercoaster of grief; initially it is every emotion experienced all at once and then once we get accustomed to it we see the life for what it was.*

*If lighting starts a fire in the forest, should we put it out?*

*People that are full of themselves have no room for anyone else and are the last to realize why they are always alone.*

*Truly creative and innovative people are never appreciated in their own time because society is not able to comprehend their offerings.*

---

*If you take the path to a green and Eco-friendly life you take the chance that ultimately in the end your life has no impact.*

*If a tree falls in the forest it will make a sound. Does it take someone to hear it justify that it was ever there? The silence of a life extinguished can still be the loudest sound imaginable.*

*Comedy is being strong enough to reveal your weaknesses.*

*Bend or break with the choices you make.*

*The people we love are a reflection of our own projection.*

*As a leader give the people what they want and be prepared to help them accept the consequences.*

*To truly appreciate the moment you need to humble yourself to it.*

*Life made simple: when you breathe just breathe. A beginning, a middle, and an end, just be prepared to breathe.*

*Make the most of every chance you have to take a breath and take the time to correct every mistake made: learn from it and teach the willing. You will exist longer deceased than you will alive so make the most of your time to make your memory worthy to survive.*

*Scientifically it is an accepted fact that the accumulated effect of a rain drop can echo for centuries. If that same rain drop falls in the lakes or oceans the effect is amplified to thousands of years. Sometimes something so small is worth emulating.*

*History repeats itself. This is what we all know, but if you pay attention to it we can learn from it and not make the same mistakes again. It repeats itself so we can learn and move forward intelligently.*

*The future is happening all around us, but interestingly, to see the past all we need to do is look up.*

*Music can be a measure of our growth.*

*The most meaningful conversations can sometimes have no words at all.*

*Overpopulated places on the planet are starving and dying for all the reasons we already have the ability to prevent and yet the wealthy throw away the excess of the day.*

*As the stable nations starve, the third world*
*we move to our own extinction.*

*The extent of life expectancy can be measured by what still holds your interest every day and when you get to the point when you begin to lose interest in your own life. The only cure is to stay interested in your own life by taking an interest and taking charge. Do not allow yourself to be a spectator in your own life; otherwise it is over.*

*True perpetual motion only happens in a lifecycle, not unlike that of the universe. It is a force of energy moving in all directions at the same time and cannot be controlled and can only continue without resistance, which are two reasons why we cannot duplicate it in its true form.*

*Don't confuse being taken for granted when the other person actually expects more.*

*We lie out loud but most often keep the truth silent.*

*True love is the keeper of your inner most secrets and the protector of your weaknesses.*

*If you find yourself spending life pursuing things that cause you great unhappiness remember that these are the moments you can never get back. Stop wasting your time.*

*Time best spent is to be the one to create worlds for others to stop, observe, experience, and live in, as it adds to the majesty of everyone's life.*

*No matter whom you are and what you know,
it's about how many you love and everyone
you know. The pain you cause or the joy you
bring it makes little difference because
everything will end up in the same place.*

*My view on life is embrace all you can the best you can. Life is truly a gift of unmatched happiness and uncertainty. The moments we have are brief and we will know far fewer people than we will ever meet. Life offers us the experience that we can never keep; knowledge is something we borrow and is meant to be passed forward. Our responsibility as we move through life is to pay forward our experience and expertise to benefit the next generation.*

*I stood at the top of a great mountain. I fell, but I never forgot what it felt like to experience the clarity and peace. Now I have true vision of where I want to be. I know the direction and I am aware of the path that will take me there.*

*Be proud of me for what I can bring that has the value of my time, caring, and creativity. Don't dwell on the material things that pretend to be important and make life necessary.*

*Every life has an effect. We all make choices that will determine how we can impact society and the betterment of all or how little we chose to change the face of the planet. You can choose to be a summer breeze, a rain drop, or a cloud. I would choose a tidal wave.*

*Find your true love and feel the freedom to release your heart and all the secrets that exists within it: pure and dark. Now that your true soul is safe and protected from outsiders reach out peacefully to the other heart.*

*If your life was a car, then happiness would be finding the perfect parking place.*

*The hand of man is no match for the finger of God.*

*A prejudice comment takes away the camouflage of your true self.*

*Stop doing the things you hate and do not pay for what you really don't need. Make sure you get full value for all you do.*

*It's only fair to be convicted of the crime you commit.*

*In modern society isolation is often confused with loneliness. Isolation is a choice and loneliness is a result.*

*Before you experience the inevitable end and you are standing close to the darkness, take the time to look into the shadows and if it offers you the chance to re-enter the light, make the most of it.*

*Choice is a matter of control, so it is a matter of choice if we wish to take it or give it.*

*The key to longevity in a relationship is to share your interests and goals so that at the end of the road, as the dust clears, it is just the two of you standing together and that you are still standing as friends.*

*There are reasons why flies don't land on
flowers. Flowers and taste being relative.*

*We are the same way as we ingest the vomit of
bees and the fluids from cows; we are not
along several species around the world who
feast on the excretions of others.*

*We are a confusing species; we have the ability to eradicate all life from a planet we don't understand and yet we fight to conserve species that are close to extinction. This alone could be causing as much damage as all our wars as the planet fights back for equilibrium. We may be saving ourselves into extinction. Keep cutting down trees until we can tax the air.*

*There are places on earth that are peaceful and pristine. They are this way because they are unexplored.*

*Parental Guidance*

*When you are young your knowledge and experiences are in an imaginary bank.  The idea is to take full advantage of education and experience and place it in this account so that later in life you can take from the knowledge bank and get further ahead. It is important to start this account at the earliest possible age to offer you the greatest chance for overall success in life and the ability to withdrawal the highest level of information throughout your life. There will come a time, as you get older, when the bank will no longer accept the information you have to offer and the account will become empty, obsolete, and out dated.*

*The reason looking back over the past mistakes, hindsight, and reflection offers the wisdom to prevent a rash decision and repeating the same mistake from happening again. It is nature's way of forcing evolution of thought.*

*The truth behind personal failure and growth is by not taking control of your situation, not moving in a direction of your own choosing, and learning from the lessons of past failure.*

*Pay it forward by treating yourself right first. Being available to others at the expense of yourself will cause your own failure as all around you succeed.*

*Every action has an equal and opposite reaction; so if you are constantly pushing people away, why are we surprised when they leave?*

*Life as we know it cannot exist in the vacuum of outer space as well as many other environments on Earth. As we find this to be true it tells me that we have a lot to learn.*

*Faith is a word we use to disguise all that is wrong with organized society and things we are not able to explain. Ultimately it is redefined over time to be made more relatable.*

*Shouldn't Faith remain constant if it is true?*

*We move forward to the unknown and invent answers based on the idea of faith and how it offers a spiritual reward for obedience, but every other form of life on our planet goes through their entire life cycle regardless of the purity of their heart and their soul. They have the same opportunity of salvation without the pressures of organized religion.*

*If there is any truth to an afterlife then it shouldn't matter what religion you follow since there is no proof of which one is the right one as they all promise salvation on their terms and the ability to repent if an individual is wrong. With all religions being without loopholes, is it not a time for us to stop, unite, and end the fight?*

*If we dream of peaceful and tranquil places, unspoiled by modern society that remain unchanged, then why are we so intent on advancing beyond our comfort zone?*

*Pockets of the human race seem to get through life happily and co-operatively. When we introduce organized living to the undeveloped areas of the world we introduce all the sins we preach to resist and they crumble due to our intervention. Undisturbed should remain undisturbed.*

*Sometimes it is better to take no steps rather than large ones or even small ones. Patience pays.*

*The human race is the only one on the planet that manufacture garbage. Well that is because we are the only species that creates anything.*

*Every species is in conflict but we are the only ones that can settle disputes through compromise and bargaining; we just choose not to, unless the price is right.*

*Mother Nature is like the common cold and as soon as we think we have an understanding of how she works in conjunction with the planet and how we can begin to predict what is over the horizon, she evolves without warning and reminds us how small we are and that we are just victims in waiting.*

*If we can put a price on anything, we will discover a way to profit or exploit it. Without value, it will remain unknown.*

*The concept of communism works. Greed and free enterprise kill co-operation.*

*The end of a life is ended when the story is finalized and the author has nothing left to write. Sometimes the footnote is sad and disjointed. It is also the one time where friends, families, and the writer himself may not have clear answers for the story's end.*

*The dead may not know how they died. The lost souls are left looking for the reasons for their demise and the living are left with questions and uncertainty.*

*Word rarely represents what the speaker really means because the agenda can be hidden in the message.*

*It's funny how the longer we are with someone the less you may really know about them, how complaisant we become, and are easily surprised by changes in their behavior.*

*Faith is a tall order when it offers a vague promise of the one thing no one can prove or offer a clear path to. We are surrounded by millions of reasons every day to prove faith is a myth when it appears that God looks the other way and allows bad things to happen to good people. Bad things happen to bad people as well, we just do not care. If Faith is the ultimate test, how will we know if we pass?*

*Heroes are the ones that act on our fears and allow us to keep them.*

## In Closing

*Science is the vehicle of discovery and knowledge but sometimes you need to question the logic of the one behind the wheel. It is thought to be useful to mine the moon and shoot missiles into it. However, the moon reflects the Earth's ability to control the tides and no one sees an issue with taking it away or physically changing the satellite. Is it really global warming due to our toxic ways, is the planet self-correcting, or are we shooting missile into the only thing that helps us maintain balance?*

*Religion and science will prove there is an afterlife and it will be based on the simplest of principals. If the energy cannot be destroyed only converted then science must discover how to identify what the energy is converted to after it goes beyond our ability to see it. Religion will be there to help us cope with the findings.*

.

www.ingramcontent.com/pod-product-compliance
Lightning Source LLC
Chambersburg PA
CBHW070524030426
42337CB00016B/2093